1

FROM
LIMITED TO
LIMITLESS

4

FROM
LIMITED TO
LIMITLESS

Deirdre Cunningham

5

6

From Limited to Limitless

Copyright © 2015
Deirdre Cunningham

Printed in the United States of America

Library of Congress – Catalogued in Publication Data

ISBN 13 978-0692743188
ISBN-10: 0692743189

Published by:
Jabez Books Writers' Agency
(A Division of Clark's Consultant Group)
www.clarksconsultantgroup.com

Jabez Books

Unless otherwise indicated all scriptural quotations are taken from the King James Version of the Bible.

A Summarized testimony

Of My Life Transformed Into A

Curse-Breaking

Legacy

Dedication

This book is dedicated to all those who are trying to overcome "self" and people issues in order to realize their divine purpose for living.

Table of Contents

Introduction   15

Chapter 1

In The Beginning   21

Chapter 2

I'm A Girl?   41

Chapter 3

Who Am I?   57

13

Chapter 4

Where Did I Come From?   79

Chapter 5

Why Am I Here?   95

Chapter 6

Where Am I Going?   115

Chapter 7

And The End Of That Man/Woman   131

Chapter 8

Conclusion   147

INTRODUCTION

*E*verything in life – starting from conception – determines whether or not you will accomplish God's goal for your life. The type of Mother you have; where your Father is from; who counsels you; what your eyes see and ears hear; what you partner and agree with; it all plays a part in how your end will be.

Will you be a model, or an actor/actress? Will you be a business owner, or the business's janitor? Will you have money, or just know people who have money? Will you own the bus company, or drive or ride the bus? Will you run the school, or be a drop out? Will you expand, or never grow?

The scary part of this is the graveyards are full of people who died too soon before realizing the answers to these questions.

So many have passed through life without recognizing and comprehending their purpose and reason for existing; why the

Lord has caused them to be. Then, they end up regretting being born and hating their existence, or living a life of failures, mishaps and mistakes, or merely existing without fulfillment.

Well, I KNOW most assuredly that a life of failure, mishaps, mistakes, unfulfillment and non-productivity is not the Lord's plan for us!

Yes, the Lord does have a predestinated and predetermined outcome for our life; but, it is through our submission and obedience to our own selfish will that we sabotage that divine outcome. We are free-will agents, which means we have the power of choice and are not forced to make the right decision.

Therefore, our *will* is what can make or break the Lord's expected end for us.

We must be able to differentiate between what is *self* will and what is *the Lord's* will in order to accomplish the success we say we desire, and most importantly what the Lord intended before the foundation of the world. Coming into this knowledge is a daily, life-long process. This process begins at birth and never ends. Hence, it can be frustrating to strive to obtain this wisdom and seem to never gain it.

Answering the questions of Who, What When, Where and Why about self will accomplish over half the battle!

You must be glad in knowing that the task ahead is NOT impossible! We must learn to master our daily instructions (eat the daily bread the Lord provides us) and keep our eyes fixed on the promised successes ahead. Then, when distractions come to jar us off course, we'll have the chutzpa to obey the Word of God: *"Submit yourselves therefore unto God. Resist the devil, and he will flee from you."* James 4:7

As you read this book which contains *a glimpse* of my personal story, I pray that you will be provoked to rediscover the "you" which the Lord predestinated you to be! Or, if you already know who you should be, I pray that you will find new inspiration to "press hard" into being that person excellently!

I beseech you to avoid reading this book in the posture of learning some darkness about me; but, rather to learn more of the enemy we all have to defeat: *self*!

CHAPTER 1

IN THE BEGINNING

A man is an awesome creature. Even God Himself is intrigued by the man He created. In so much that the angels marveled saying *"What is man that thou art mindful of him."* Hebrews 2:6

Adding to that, a military man is an outstanding man! He's poised, confident, strong in character, and can and will endure as much as necessary to accomplish his mission!

He recognizes that people around him look up to and lean on him. Therefore, his steps are careful but precise so as to avoid casualties while moving forward. Yet, he recognizes he must look to an authority higher than himself for instructions and guidance along his life's path if he is to be successful in his endeavors.

Right along beside him is the auspiciousness of a woman. She carries a heavy load - whether single or married, with or without children - but the weight of the load never hinders her steps!

She's wise, but not conniving; cunning but not sly. She's rich in a lot of things, but being poor has pleasure for her as well! She's misunderstood, yet understanding. She's delicate but will conquer a dare. She causes her surroundings to adapt to her and the needs of those who concern her.

This was the kind of man and woman I had for a father and mother.

If ever anything happened that he didn't plan, I don't remember it because he was always cool and nothing seemed to discourage him.

To top it off, they were God fearing people! My father was a singer in a group and a deacon in the church; and my mother was a teacher of the scriptures. Boy could my Daddy sing! And boy could my mother orate!

My father was my hero! No harm could come to me because he was my father! He was strong in body and will. Whatever he decided was going to be, that's exactly what was!

If ever anything happened that he didn't plan, I don't remember it because he was always *cool* and nothing seemed to discourage him.

My mother was a *beautiful lady* to me. Everything about her was perfect in my eyes. She strove for excellence in everything she did. The fact that she couldn't cook I didn't know until she started inferring it as I got older.

She was resourceful in that whatever she had, that was what she (and we) used and made it work. In addition, I thought my mother knew *everything*! I learned from my mother to treat people respectfully, to love nice things and take care of them so they will last a long time, and "do all things decently and what?" ["...*in order*" was the response of the child(ren) she was chastening for doing something wrong] LOL! (I know my Siblings remember that!)

Now, as a young child I really lived a life of fun and adventure. I was one who loved to flip, turn and jump. I mimicked my brother no matter what he did! If he jumped, flipped, did a handstand, or turned in circles, I was right with him doing the same thing. (I guess that's where my competitive nature began.) In that, I was just like my brother in my mind.

So, jumping off roofs, climbing through windows and playing with frogs were things I thought I was supposed to do. I thought my sisters were weird and wimpy because they were too *girly* for these kinds of things.

I loved to play in the dirt; and eating some mud pie was part of my daily activities! Nothing like that Mississippi mud!

I didn't really like dolls, publicly that is, until I started getting them for Christmas. (Strange, huh! What girl doesn't like dolls?)

But, there was one particular doll I got for Christmas one year that I always slept with and she stayed on my bed. I even made up my bed often so she would have a nice place to stay until I got back in the bed.

If I discovered this doll was off my bed and on the floor somehow, there was a problem and someone had better provide answers!

Thank you Daddy for refusing to stop buying me dolls for Christmas! ;-)

Regardless of my peculiar personality, my parents knew there was something special about me! They each would talk to me about growing up to be somebody in life. (They talked to all *four* of us about growing up and becoming somebody; especially when we were "clowning!"☺)

I was certainly special alright!

I remember, when going to take my kindergarten graduation picture, my mother and siblings asked me did I want them to go inside with me to take the picture. I replied, "No." as I sashayed away from them and walked into the building.

I took the picture and walked out to join my family and get in the car.

I guess it must have happened too quickly to them because they asked in amazement, "Are you finished?" I replied, "Yes" in a manner to say to them I didn't know what else they expected, and got in the car like I had everything under control! (*I'm Shaking My Head thinking about this* because I was a mess!*)

My mother made certain she exposed us to as much culture enrichment as her resources could afford. We seemed to be musically inclined, so we were being instructed to play woodwind instruments.

was my thinking now.

Now, in my mind, I was ready for the big leagues!

I wanted to be independent so badly until I thought taking this picture without a guide proved I was ready to take on everything that my siblings, and my parents, had been handling before this time. "I can do it all by myself!"

Yes, this is when my 'n*othing's impossible'* attitude began to develop!

However, strange, unhappy events took place in my family when I was between seven and twelve years old

My mother made certain she exposed us to as much culture enrichment as her resources could afford. We seemed to be musically inclined, so we were being instructed to play woodwind instruments.

Therefore, every summer my brother and oldest sister went to orchestra camp. My mother drove us there and back while my father stayed behind working two jobs.

We were headed down the road on the two-hour journey as we had become used to doing. I, being seven years old at the time, became antsy and wouldn't be still.

I remember my mother looking back at me, scolding me and telling me to sit down about three times.

When my mother turned forward the third time, the oncoming car startled her and she lost control of the car trying to dodge that accident.

Once the car stopped, the car was in a ditch on the opposite side of the road, glass was broken everywhere, my sisters were crying, and my mother was telling everyone to calm down.

I was fine, to me, until I saw my brother was not opening his eyes and a cow was licking at his head!

I kept screaming "Is my brother okay? What's wrong with my brother?" all the way to the hospital; and even while being taken to get a few stitches on my face and leg.

I kept screaming "Is my brother okay? What's wrong with my brother?" all the way to the hospital; and even while being taken to get a few

35

It ended up that, because my brother was asleep before the accident, he was unconscious from being knocked around during the accident. My mother had a dislocated hip and the rest of us had minor cuts and bruises.

I remember feeling responsible, guilty and afraid once we got home. *"If only I had just sat down like my mother told me to!"*

I remember feeling responsible, guilty and afraid once we got home. "If only I had just sat down like my mother told me to!" I didn't even realize my own

I didn't even realize my own pain of having stitches in my face.

At least, not until my father, being so angry that something happened to us in his absence, took out his pocket knife and cut out the stitches claiming the doctors didn't know what they were talking about.

I can still hear him when he said, "You were supposed to be my model. MMMM...m." He was really hurt!
Only a few years after this, my mother and father were divorced. I remember feeling numb and in denial.

I didn't know how to feel or think toward my father because I was confused. It wasn't that

> *We were the perfect family in my eyes and nothing like this was supposed to happen to our family. Other people's families, but not to ours!*

my mother said anything bad or influenced us against my father. I just really didn't know how I was supposed to respond!

We were the perfect family in my eyes and nothing like this was supposed to happen to our family. Other people's families, but not to ours!

I remember fear gripping me terribly one afternoon when my father came home after learning we had come home from school.

From time to time, we and my mother would leave the house for some days and then return home. I know now that it was because my mother was preparing for their divorce.

From time to time, we and my mother would leave the house for some days and then return home. I know now that it was because my mother was preparing for their divorce.

This time, when my father learned my youngest sister and I had returned home after school, he left work and came home to see us because he missed us.

The absence of my father made me feel vulnerable, unprotected and alone.

I don't know why, but I was so afraid of him until I told my sister we needed to hide under the kitchen table!

Sidebar: I understand now that Divorce is the result of someone being selfish and set on having their way. That's for real!

As a result of the divorce, the absence of my father made me feel vulnerable, unprotected and alone.

Who will fight for me now? Who will protect me now? Who will hug me, make it all go away and make me feel better now?

I guess I will!

Ahh, the formative Years...should be strategic, never haphazard!

What was your beginning like?

NOTES

CHAPTER 2

I'M A GIRL?

I was in sixth grade at Power Elementary School. Emily Greener was the principal. I knew this because my mother, being a Southern-raised, family oriented woman, made herself known at the school and made certain she knew all the staff, especially the principal.

My mother's usual statement was "If you ever have AAAANY trouble, call me." Well, needless to say, I strove HARD to make sure my mother never got *one* phone call!

This particular day, I had just finished lunch and was going to the bathroom. I was focused on how much fun I would have outside in a few minutes because after lunch was recess!

As I was walking, I heard "psst!" I turned around, and to my surprise, it was a boy trying to get my attention! I was INSTANTLY nervous!

Now mind you, I had witnessed boyfriend/girlfriend relationships among my two older siblings; but, it didn't faze me because it was engraved in my mind that I wasn't even *close* to old enough to have a boyfriend. So, dirt was my friend…up to this point, that is!

But, oh my goodness! There's a boy trying to get *my* attention! I think? I looked around me as if to ask him who he was talking to. He said, "You!"
Huh?
Then, he winked at me!

Now wait just one minute! Boys don't like me! Not one boy has ever looked at me as being interested in me before now! I haven't really looked at any *boy* before now either!

I'm a tomboy for real – girl-who-climbs-trees-and-jumps-cars tomboy! Are you *sure* you like *me*?

So, I turned around again, questioning him with my expression

> *That's when my eyes were opened, and I realized I was a girl who a boy could like!*

whether or not he was talking to me. He winked again!

That's when my eyes were opened, and I realized I was a girl who a boy *could* like!

Oh boy! From that day forward it was on! I began to try and dress like a *girl*, even like I actually *cared* about how I looked! Now that a boy liked me, I had to really lay it on with my looks! You know, like my oldest sister did! At least that's how it seemed to me.

But, how do I do that? I don't have her clothes, her body or her brains!

Well, I'll do as my mother did: use what I got and make it work! Nah!

With all this attention flowing my way, my motivation for everything I did became getting rave reviews

So now, instead of just grabbing clothes and putting them on, I started trying to make sure everything matched and fit in the right places. Yeah, that ought to do it! ;-)

With all this attention flowing my way, my motivation for everything I did became getting rave reviews. But when I think about it, I already had *this* motivation in motion.

Not many years before this, around the third or fourth grade, while briefly at a different school, my class was putting on a play. The only character in the play I remember is the monster. That's because I volunteered to draw that monster.

While drawing the monster, I envisioned the principal and my mother being emotionally moved to tears at how good the drawing was. (*Geesh,* what brought *that thought* on?)

After the play when the principal and my mother were in conversation and spoke of the monster (which was the star of the play, if you ask me; and, I was now holding in my hand because I was taking it home), the principal remarked, "Yes, Deirdre is very talented as she drew this monster for the play!" My mother merely replied, "Yes, she's a really gifted child."

I was thinking, "*Wow! This is it! Here come the tears!*" Then,...they conversed a little more and the conversation was over; then, we walked away.

What? That's it? No Tears! No Emotion! No bragging! Now, what's *really* going on?

> *I was lost in my own thoughts of never being good enough!*

Although this moment was sort of a big letdown, I continued to *pre-meditate* outcomes of my actions; and I continued to be disappointed.

So, now you understand why the boy winking at me was such a major event. Before that happened, I was lost in my own thoughts of never being good enough! Somewhere in me I had come to the conclusion that I was not going to be well-liked, find true love, or get a lot of gifts. I even considered myself ugly.

Incidents like the monster *flop* had occurred one time too many for me; so, I began to put forth less effort. At least until this *boy* came along!

I came home that day he winked at me looking like I had a secret that was worth a million dollars and you should want to know what it was. I was grinning from ear to ear!

My sister noticed (it's not like it was hard to see!) and blurted out in front of everybody, "Deirdre, what are you cheesing about?" I just looked at her, slightly dropped my smile and gave a sort of snarling glare because I didn't want *everyone* to know my secret!

When we got in our room, my sister asked me again. I said, "This boy at school winked at me today!" My sister laughed as if I had told a really good joke.

I yelled, "For real!" I yelled because she had to stop laughing since this was serious business: I had to know how to be *like her* to keep him interested in me; otherwise, my dream wouldn't come to pass!

You know the dream that the first person you fall in love with will marry you, you'll have amazing children, and you all will be the envy of everyone around you!

Seeing how serious I was about this, my sister stopped laughing and we began to have a sister-to-sister chat. You know:

what's his name, how does he look, do you like him, etc.

Later in the year, my family came to pick me up from school. As I got in the car, they had seen me with the boy. Not touching each other or anything like that! After all, this was a new twist in my personality, so I was taking it slow – *very* slow!

When I got in the car, my older sister and brother asked "Is that him?" I proudly said, "Yes!" They both burst into laughter and said, "Girl, he fat!" I immediately froze in my mind.

What? He's fat? Really? I didn't even notice *that*! Hmm. I pondered their ridicule for a few minutes more.

Then, I quickly shouted back "SO!" I thought in my mind: I don't see nobody else beating down the *Deirdre*-door! I can just feel safe with him, since he's bigger than me, and[23] squeeze him like a teddy bear!

There it was! I'm a girl falling for a *fat* boy and I don't care who doesn't like or makes fun of it!

He's a *boy* and he likes me – that's all that matters.

Reflection is GREAT.....when it's positive!
Write three most meaningful, positive memories of your early life.

NOTES

CHAPTER 3

WHO AM I?

Well, of course the "fat boy" craze opened the door to being boy crazy! Seemed like I set out on a quest to get the most popular boy to like me!

I gradually went from being a tomboy and shamefaced, to looking for my Romeo, my

> *I began to be in a self-created storm of trying to measure up to a standard I perceived to exist.*

rescuer, my lover who would make everyone take notice of me and see that I'm worth more than all or most have entreated me to be.

I began to be in a self-created storm of trying to measure up to a standard I perceived to exist.

I *must* be cute enough, smart enough, *easy* enough, understanding enough, talented enough, giving enough to meet the mark and pass the girl-who-will-be-his-girlfriend-then-wife test.

Oh yes! I could see it all working out....eventually! One day, I'll meet him. He'll come to my church and say he came to get me and marry me. Then, we'll be the admired couple in church with the beautiful children, house, car and family.

I didn't realize I had inducted myself into this "game" that's played until your heart is broken, your dreams are shattered and your mind is confused.

Yet, I didn't realize I had inducted myself into this "game" that's played until your heart is broken, your dreams are shattered and your mind is confused.

65

What was confusing is I still maintained that I was in control and knew exactly what I was doing with myself! No one could fool me or get over on me because I was the game master and in control of me and the game I was playing!

I was in the game called "Give Away All Of You And Get Nothing In Return!" And that's exactly what I did!

This game took me so far until I became

I was in the game called "Give Away All Of You And Get Nothing In Return!" And that's exactly what I did!

addicted to sex through the strong force of loneliness and depression.

The people around me didn't know I was depressed and extremely lonely because I was always the life of the party! I entered the room loud and full of laughter most of the time. When I wasn't that way, I was extremely silent and angry. I was always one extreme or the other.

And, BOY did I have a mouth on me! Sometimes my mouth was filthy, when no adults were around, of course, and always loud. If others were afraid to say it, I would say it! I grew fearless and would jump at a challenge no matter how dangerous it appeared to be.

Once, a family friend was over our house visiting briefly with my brother. I was always very playful with him; but, this time I went overboard. I went into a taunting mode with him.

He kept telling me to stop; but, I heard that as a challenge and kept going.

He swiftly turned around to me, put his hands around my neck and said, "Girl, I'll choke you!" He began to squeeze my neck until I could feel my blood circulation in my head stopping.

I just looked at him as if to say, "Go ahead." In my mind, I remember thinking "*I don't want to live anyway.*"

The "game" had such a grip on me until I began to want to commit suicide.

He kept squeezing until he got scared and said, "GIRL!" as he released my neck and stepped back from me as if he had seen a ghost.

I just stood there looking at him as he left out of the door. The "game" had such a grip on me until I began to want to commit suicide. The only thing that stopped me was I knew I would go to hell if I killed myself; and after all that I had suffered, I certainly didn't want hell to be my reward!

I began to write awful letters about myself and leave them in places where I knew my family would find them. I wanted to provoke my family to send me away or do something awful to me so I would have an apparent reason to be the way I was.

My negative attitude toward myself sometimes caused those around me to respond negatively toward me.

I began to write awful letters about myself and leave them in places where I knew my family would find them. I wanted to provoke my family to send me away or do something awful to me so I would have an apparent reason to be the way I was.

I was so daring! But, I had two major turning points!

ONE: While in high school, a fancy, fine looking guy came to the school just looking around. When we finally caught eyes (as I was trying not to but trying to get his attention), he asked me did I want to go with him.

Being in the state I was in, my desperation drowned my intelligence and I told him yes.

Now, mind you, I had never seen this guy before a day in my life! What's worse is I wasn't scared!

We went to the mall as any girl my age would have wanted to do. My daring self went to the mall near my house though! (Why wasn't I thinking that my mother could catch me there? She didn't though. That's because Jesus wanted me to live! ☺)

He bought me a top, a pair of pants and a CHEAP flower/rose. Then, he took me home. Yep that's right: no sex! (The "no sex" part was the set-up to make it easy for sex later!)

When I got home and my mother asked where I had been, I told her all my *"wonderful"* news of this guy and my *"gentleman"* encounter. But, I told the story as if my mother would be impressed!

To my surprise, my mother hit the roof exclaiming how crazy that was and how something could have happened to me.

To my surprise, my mother hit the roof exclaiming how crazy that was and how something could have happened to me without anyone knowing it! But, I truly didn't expect her response because I was so caught up in my fantasy of an approved prince charming coming to rescue me, the princess!

My mother's truth opened my eyes to the fact that I had really lost control of myself and was headed nowhere fast! *Who in the world am I?*

The next evening, my mother reported to me that she had investigated the guy and found out his real name, where he was from, and that he had a misdemeanor record. Her summary of him made me realize how stupid I was once again! Unfortunately, *that's* when I realized something bad could have happened to me!

Now, wasn't I embarrassed! You don't make me look stupid to anyone, especially not my mother – the one I'm trying so hard to impress! So, that *craze*, if you will, was immediately over!

I was so not-in-control until I didn't have one clue of what I was going to do with myself.

I was so *not*-in-control until I didn't have one clue of what I was going to do with myself when I graduated from High School.

Thanks to my mother's intellectual associations, I got a full scholarship to a junior college majoring in voice, the *only* thing I had going for myself at the time!

TWO: While away from home in College, I had "friends" who would leave campus most weekends and come back to my home town. Since my newest boyfriend was there, of course I went along for the ride and got dropped off at his house.

Well, all of that promiscuity (and rebellion and disobedience) afforded me a baby growing in my womb!

Now, I don't know about you, but my mother was a no-nonsense woman. Therefore, I actually believed she would LITERALLY kill me for becoming pregnant before marriage! So, the thought of telling her I was pregnant literally horrified me!

> I was Cute, Cool Outside, Sad Within, AND Christ-less! #TNT COMBO!

Nonetheless, I had determined in myself a long time before that, if I did get pregnant while unmarried, I would do whatever it took

> *I did finally bite the bullet and tell my mother that I was pregnant. **That was one of the worse days of my life.***

to take care of my child myself! I did finally bite the bullet and tell my mother that I was pregnant. **That was one of the worse days of my life because I had terribly hurt my mother**, and that was absolutely not what I wanted to do!

But, that's not the worse part – the #TWO awakening!

Around my sixth month, I had come home because I had been talking to the other responsible party about us getting married.

After all, that's what we were going to do anyway, right?

He came to the house and I let him in the front to sit and wait to talk to my mother, to ask her if he could marry me like the gentleman he was...*right*!

I left out of the front room and went to my mother in the kitchen to ask her to come in to talk to him. I said, "Mother, could you come in the front so he can talk to you?" She said, "For what?!" I said, "He wants to ask you if he can marry me." She was livid! She raised her voice and said, "You think he's going to marry you?!!"

Now, her words slapped me in the face with the truth: as nervous as he was acting, my mother may be right! But, no she can't be right! Nobody makes a fool out of me. I've got this down packed and I know whether or not somebody's trying to make a fool out of me! I'm too smart to be made a fool of! Right?

Well, low and behold, my mother *was* right! This same guy who I let tell me that the reason he was standing in the cold at the football game huddled up with *another girl* was because she and I made him feel the same way, has now made me look ridiculously stupid in front of my mother, *and* left me with a baby!

How in the world could this be? May I please just go back to the days before the *fat boy* craze and start all over???

Is starting over not a part of life? I can't just wipe all of these crazy mistakes I've made away and start from scratch? Maybe I can change my reputation and my name so I'll become the person everyone wanted and expected me to be?

This can't be happening to me! I'm pregnant, unmarried, miserable, feeling hopeless and extremely embarrassed once again! I think this is when the phrase began being spoken to me: "You're not going to be much unless you change!"

Being in search of "the one" who would make the difference in my life and cause everything to turn around, I became a slave to a lot of wrong things!

Oh, most certainly I was in church – born and raised Baptist, sang in the choir - even lead a song occasionally – and was there whenever the doors were opened *literally*! [Siblings, what's the reply when we would ask if we were going to church? "If you live! You plan on living don't you?"]

But, *Christ Jesus* wasn't in me; *church* was! But, "church" alone wouldn't destroy what was inside of me.

At this point, I didn't want "church"; I wanted "me" back because *obviously* I had lost myself!

Who I have become at this point is definitely *not* who I am! Is it?

Somebody please tell me *Who Is Deirdre*?

Thinking is good for your soul!......and everyone around you!

What event(s) in your life caused you to stop and think?

NOTES

CHAPTER 4

WHERE DID I COME FROM?

Being pregnant without a hope of immediate marriage in sight really punched me in my gut hard enough to make me stop what I had been doing and think!

Where did this person I had become actually come from? What happened to the person I seemed to be in the beginning?

How did I get in this position? Where did my youthful, joyful life go? May I just start this over? May I be innocent again?

Being unmarried and pregnant forced me to try and grow up fast: I was determined not to be an *ignorant*, *ghetto* mother!

I was not going to have my baby dragging behind me looking thrown away while I looked all glamorous.

I also got slapped in the face with the fact that, however I was while carrying my baby, that's the same way my baby would be once born. So, I really began to honestly analyze myself.

What in the world makes me so angry until I won't accept help from those who try to help me, yet I want help – help with myself and help with my life?

From where did I develop this self-hatred? What are the things that have caused me to be the person I had become? How could I have such positive views of everyone except myself?

During my grade school years while being in utter misery most of the time, for some reason I looked up my name – Deirdre – in the dictionary, trying to make sense of why I felt the way I did about myself and treated myself with such carelessness. Hopefully, knowing this would give me a solution to whatever my problem was.

I found out that *Deirdre* is French and means sorrow; *Deirdre* was a damsel who, upon learning her fiancé was killed in battle, committed suicide.

Unfortunately, once I learned what my name meant, rather than having a solution to my problem as I had hoped, I gained a reason to be the same or worse in my problem and became a partner of the devil's plight to lay sadness and depression on me thick.

The voice of satan magnified, telling me that I was not worth much, I wasn't meant to have friends, I was a mistake to my parents, I was *supposed* to be sad and depressed; I should just hope to die and maybe people will be sad enough to have a funeral for me.

While in college, I became the president of the choir, and our choir toured the East Coast in which I had a solo that was featured during the tour. I was the first of my siblings to graduate from college and have a degree, and I graduated with honors!

Yet, the negative, demeaning voice that spoke to me on a regular basis was greater than my accomplishments

You would think I realized greatness and happiness was for me when I sat next to Andrew Young!

and I couldn't find satisfaction or self fulfillment.

Therefore, after learning the meaning of my name, I wondered who would name me this name, knowing what it meant? Why give me this name if you wanted me to live? (Isn't that just like the devil to try and blame someone else for your own actions, feelings and ill beliefs?) What's worse yet is I was made to feel that I was adopted and not the natural child of my parents. (How can *that* be when I act just like my father and look like my mother?)

These are all part of the plan of the enemy to divide (me away from those who truly loved and cared about me) and conquer (me in my own mind, thoughts and feelings so that I would result to drastic/devastating measures, such as self mutilation or suicide)!

My unplanned pregnancy caused me to care enough for my unborn baby until I actually began to slightly care about myself.

THANK YOU JESUS FOR ALLOWING ME TO GET PREGNANT SO ALL OF THE DEVIL'S PLANS WOULD CEASE AND DESIST!

Suddenly, I cared enough about me to not crave sex and be able to say "No" to guys who just wanted my body!

I didn't want to get drunk to drown away my sorrows anymore! I didn't hope someone would run me over to take me away from this world anymore! I no longer felt the need to smoke all the marijuana I could in one sitting to numb myself of the hurt, pain and disappointments I encountered!

Better yet, I began to actually, for the first time in my life, think I was cute! (Imagine that! I really never gave it thought before.)

I resisted feeling lonely, depressed, sad, hated, bitter…just so that my baby wouldn't feel that from me and become worse than I used to be! (That's right: the *bad* personality in you is duplicated, and *worse,* in your offspring, and continues to multiply worse in each generation...until it is stopped, that is!)

As I began this quest of self-ensued change, I came to comprehend that some of my personality and attitudes were generational.

My primary concern was for my baby! My sister says that, at that time, there was an R&B song out that had in the lyrics "...thank you for my son/child"; and when she heard the song, she thought of me. Um. Ok!

Well, I never knew that song because I had stopped listening to a mixture of music in an effort to set a more holy precedence for my baby; but, I was truly thankful for my child!

As I began this quest of self-ensued change, I came to comprehend that some of my personality and attitudes were generational. I found myself as Isaiah did in Chapter 6, verse 5: *"Then said I, Woe is me! For I am undone; because I am a man of unclean lips, and I dwell in the midst of a people of unclean lips: for mine eyes have seen the King, the Lord of hosts."*

These character flaws had caused families to become divided from each other in heart. The families that I grew up knowing had become broken, bitter and bruised.

Well, when my eyes became open to this fact, I made up my mind I wasn't going to be the same miserable, sad, lonely person I had been!

Standing out above the rest should benefit others and be worth mimicking! What are your character flaws that you must destroy and replace?

NOTES

101

CHAPTER 5

WHY AM I HERE?

That ONE decision caused me to begin to pull *myself* out of the pit I had allowed myself to be cast down into.

I stopped being so edgy *all* the time. I laughed a lot more often than I frowned or became angry. I didn't feel slighted or cheated as much. It seemed that I became a joy to be around again. I really felt good....INSIDE!

Before this time, most people, including myself, would look at my life's experiences as tragic and unfortunate. But, I learned to appreciate the positive outcomes those experiences were capable of causing me to have!

My new way of thinking caused me to be a person who only wanted the Lord, and the Lord alone to be pleased with me. So, I no longer wanted to dance the way I used to dance – provocative, sexy and inviting. I wanted the way I moved my body to be a movement that the Lord would be *comfortable* with.

This led up to the day I sought the Lord for and received the gift of the Holy Ghost: May 2nd, 1985, round about midnight! I had on a 3-piece, gray/pastel pink suit. It was a Thursday evening in the living room of the home of one of the Mother's of the church I was attending.

The Lord Jesus laid me down in some clouds! (That's actually what I saw in my mind as I went to the floor!) When I came to myself, my tongue was moving but it wasn't because I was controlling it – the Lord had given me a language called the unknown tongue!

I remember thinking: "IT'S REAL? You *can* be filled with the Holy Spirit and speak in tongues as the Spirit of the Lord gives you utterance?" AB-SO-LUTE-LY!

I stood to my feet somehow. Then,.........I began to dance a dance that was truly *comfortable* with the Lord!

BOY, was I happy! I wanted to tell the whole world, literally, about this experience and how real it is!

That's not all!

I had heard it sung in church when I was younger "I looked at my hands and they looked new. I looked at my feet and they did too." This came back to my mind at this time.

Guess what? I looked down at my hands and they *really did look new!* I looked further down at my feet and they *really did look new too!* I started dancing all over again!

And yet more discovery was, when I walked outside, the whole world looked new – as if I had been gone away from the world for a long time and was just returning to the world and experiencing a different place.

When I got home that night, I called my aunt, not realizing it was past midnight, and tried to tell her I was filled with the Holy Ghost, but started

speaking in tongues while trying to talk to her!

ABSOLUTELY AMAZING! Me, the one whom *they* said would be "the one" had become *the one*! And, not only was I *the one*, but I had received my answer for my life-long problem of sadness and depression! The Lord has proved to me that I am lovable and worth loving!

Now, I must do something to show Him that I appreciate what He has done! What can I do? How may I show Him?

But wait! What's this? Wouldn't you know it: just when I'm set on a path toward total, inner happiness, something started to stir up that old person!

I started *reverting* (if you will) and acting like the person the Lord had saved me from! The only difference now is this *new* old person was worse than the old person! Instead of just being angry, I would be angry and disappear for long hours. Instead of just being quiet, I would be vengeful and yelling at people! Now, *who* is this new person and *where* did she come from?

In the midst of this, because of God's grace and mercy the Lord afforded me memorable experiences with Him!

Once, I was at this church we fellowshipped with often. The men there were very flirtatious and I had grown tired of encountering their lustful approaches.

I was asked to sing a solo. Usually, when I finished singing I would dance before the Lord. So, as I went up to sing, in my heart I asked the Lord to let me dance in Him before those men in such a way that they would *know* I belonged to the Lord and was off limits to them!

Well, sure enough, I sang my song; and, as usual, when I finished singing I began to dance.

As I danced, I noticed I no longer felt my feet. With my eyes closed, I looked and saw two angels – one holding each of my arms – lifting me off the floor! OH MY GOD!

When I totally grasped what was happening, the angels flew away (in the same manner as some of the angels flew away in the movie *Angels In The Outfield*; so, I *know* the writer of that movie had a divine experience!) -- Raw, divine encounters like that I will *never* forget!

Nevertheless, the *new*, old person continued off and on for a few years, although I had received *my answer* (the Holy Ghost); until one day I put on the breaks!

I grew tired of acting like I had no sense at all! I was tired of not acting like an adult and acting worse than my own child!

One day I made a bold, declarative statement to the person around me at that time, "Look! You can keep acting like that if you want to! But, from now on, I *choose* to be happy! I'm not going to keep going in these circles any longer! And, you can join me if you want to!"

From that point on, there was no more *reverting* to acting like the person I hated! Also, the further away from *that* person (the old me) I got, the more I had sweet experiences with the Lord!

I moved into my own place with my son, bought my second car without a co-signer, enjoyed my first concert as a gospel singer, and lived peaceably! I remained single with the Lord for 9 ½ years!

No, living alone wasn't the easiest thing to do! But, I resolved within myself that it was the least I could do to express to the Lord my appreciation for what He had done for me: He took all the hurt and pain away!

Then, the Lord sent me the answer to my prayer: *"Lord, whoever my husband is, let him be one who loves You as much, or more than, I do!"* And, *Truly* (like my friend says) [49] my husband is that one!

Not only that, but he also is the fleshly representation of who the Lord was to me in the Spirit before I became a natural wife.

However, about six years into our marriage I noticed that some *new* old feelings of sadness and anxiety were overcoming me from time to time. *New* because they were worse – stronger than before. I was responding to my husband and family out of the memory of my past bad experiences. Therefore, I began to question the Lord of where this was coming from and why wasn't this done with.

One day while at my kitchen sink and washing dishes before leaving for service, I looked on the widow seal over the sink.

There sat a cup my mother had sent me as a gift from my son for Mother's Day. The cup had my name - Deirdre – and the meaning – *sorrow*. I felt my spirit begin to drop as if I was supposed to respond that way.

Immediately, before I could give vent to that feeling, the Lord spoke and said, "But, I changed your name *without* changing your name." This meant my name that was on my birth certificate had not changed; yet, the Lord had given me a new name. His soft voice promptly reminded me that I was no longer *that Deirdre*, yet my name was still Deirdre!

Aha! THIS is my purpose for living! THIS is the reason God created me!

My Mantra:
I **Choose** To Be Happy!

This is why I have experienced and survived everything that happened to me in my life!

My divine purpose in life is to represent to all that the Lord has the power to reverse any negative and change it into a positive by His power and His own will! Not *Sorrow*, but Gladness!

This revelation has also caused me to realize that some of my personality woes are due to the fact that I had become so accustomed to feeling angry, being mean, and frowning until it almost felt strange and unnatural to smile, have fun, and enjoy life!

Having my understanding enlightened of my outer and inner struggles caused me to develop a watchful eye for that same self-destructive attitude in others and a love for the deliverance of others with the same struggles.

Furthermore, after a lifetime of feelings of sadness and depression within, I am finally happy inside *for real*! I enjoy life and people because I **choose** to be happy and love the privilege to do so, given to me by Jesus Himself!

Now, since I have a *purpose* for living, I will live and not die – to decree the goodness of the Lord to the entire world!

*The world will
be glad to meet
you when you
learn Who you are
introducing!*
What have you
discovered is your
divine purpose for
living?

NOTES

CHAPTER 6

WHERE AM I GOING?

Since my purpose in life has been revealed, it's time for me to run with it, isn't it? Aren't I supposed to go into all the world and tell them about Jesus' amazing, saving grace and mercy? I'm supposed to tell all I meet about my experience and new life in Jesus, right?

But, where do I go? And, what do I say when I get there? How do I know who to talk to?

Okay, maybe now is the time for me to go back around the people who knew me before my change to spread the news that my change can be everyone's change…right?. Or, maybe I will go and witness of Jesus to my abusers, the ones who disappointed me, overlooked me, and forsook me?

Well, having all this *zeal* to run for Jesus and no knowledge of where to go showed me that I needed to learn quite a few things before I was "off and running" to tell people about Jesus!

First, I had to learn that not everyone is going to receive me or what I have to say. Not everyone will care to hear about how the

Lord has blessed me. They don't care that I am no longer who I used to be.

Knowing this helped to keep me from being disappointed or feeling like a failure when rejection happened.

Second, I had to develop patience. I had to learn to wait on the Lord's instruction for witnessing to people.

Once, I was riding home on the bus and I saw a woman whose right side of her face was disfigured. I immediately thought to tell her that *my Jesus* would heal her – I believed that there was *absolutely nothing* that Jesus[55] wouldn't or couldn't do if we asked Him to do it!

When I was getting off the bus, I gave her a note I had written before getting up from my seat that said, "Jesus will heal you! You may call me if you want to, and *My name and phone number.*"

The young lady did call me later that evening, to my surprise! She was slightly flustered as people had done similar to her in times past, but as a joke.

I explained to her that it wasn't a joke; and, I know she doesn't know me, but I would never joke like that. I continued to express to her that I truly believed that Jesus would heal her then invited her to visit the church I attended.

The young lady calmed down and expressed her appreciation for my concern. But, I never saw her again.

Did her not coming to church mean that I had failed in my witness? Did I offend her and turn her away from "my Jesus" all together? What went wrong?

Absolutely nothing!

Paul tells us in the scripture that *"I have plant, Apollos watered; but God gave the increase."*1 Corinthians 3:6 This means that I may not cause the person to come to Christ; another may not cause the person to come to Christ; but just rest assured that God is in charge and His work shall be accomplished as He sees fit!

> *Once I fully consume this concept, then the Lord will give me direction for fulfilling His will; and I will become a better source of enlightenment for those purposed to follow the Christ in me.*

Therefore, I learned to not be consumed with myself, who I am, who I'm trying to be, or who I'm destined to become.

"I" really don't matter in the work of the Lord. I am merely an instrument being used by the Master.

No, that's not a "modest" thing to say to impress the hearers. That's for real! We are supposed to be instruments constantly available to be used by Jesus for His good pleasure.

Once I fully consume this concept, then the Lord will give me direction for fulfilling His will; and I will become a better source of enlightenment for those purposed to follow the Christ in me.

Here's an example: My husband and I were pastoring for about 4 or 5 years. I was very enthusiastic about leading the women of the ministry (we only had 4 at that time) and thought I could do a good job if my husband would just release me to do so.

One night, I dreamt I was leading the four women of our ministry around the city. I had a specific destination and believed I was in route to get there. However, we kept ending up at our starting point, in a complete circle. Upon ending up at the starting point the third time, I said "Wait a minute! We just came from here! I know (that) I know which way to go! Why do we keep coming back here?" When I looked at the women, they all looked at me as if to say "We're following you." Then, I woke up.

The Lord was showing me that I had these women following me as I desired, but didn't know how to take them anywhere or where the destination was! "You have them following you...Now what? Where are you going?" are the questions that were on my mind when I woke up.

Oh, how lost and bewildered I felt! The Lord had allowed His permissive will to show me that it wasn't my husband who was holding me back; it was my own ignorant (lack of knowledge) zeal that was hindering my forward motion.

I tell you I was a repentant sista! Do ya feel me?

I began to humble myself and learn from my husband how to lead. He was able to teach and pour into me. He was able to mold me into

> *I began to humble myself and learn from my husband how to lead. He was able to teach and pour into me. He was able to mold me into that vessel that God had showed him I was to become!*

that vessel that God had showed him I was to become!

Yes, *my husband* was able to teach and pour into me; not God alone!

If I was going to be pleasing to the Lord in every area of my life as I said I desired, I had to accept the methods and people with which the Lord chose to mold me into His image and make me pleasurable to Him!

So, I couldn't be as others I observed and have my ear open to any voice other than that which the Lord has ordained – like it or not!

In *this*, I recognized that He called me to be a Generational Curse Breaker for my bloodline!

How so? Well, I realized through this compelling self-illumination that I came from a generation of women who were divorced, or women who were not completely open to people and/or their husbands leading them!

From that moment, I set it in my heart and mind that I was going to be a teachable and submissive woman towards everyone – especially toward my husband!

Through that attitude, I saw the yoke of divorce began to break off my immediate family: my oldest sister got married to her *true* love, my brother found his *queen*, and my youngest sister is bringing order and direction to her life through seeking the Lord first!

I've found that God is so sovereign and infinitely wise until He will deliver you from the "effects" of those experiences in life that seemed were going to destroy you; then, uses those same experiences to anoint you to destroy yokes and free captives…starting with yourself!

Once the Lord opened my eyes and ears to myself, I was also open to hear His voice interpret to me my divine purpose: *"…he hath sent me to bind up the broken hearted."* Isaiah 61:1

Awesome! Now, I have direction for my life! I have purpose, zeal *and* knowledge. What more do I need?

*You can only
successfully
possess the land
the Lord says is
yours!*
What is your field
of harvest for your
purpose for living?

NOTES

CHAPTER 7

AND THE END OF THAT MAN & WOMAN

"So the Lord blessed the latter end of Job more than his beginning." **Job 42:11**

Well, with the knowledge of God's divine purpose for my life, I have to know that I have become formative again; but spiritually now, which is the foundation for a beautiful relationship with the Lord *and* people.

There's much more I have to learn and understand, of course. But, there's good news even in that: I will learn and become perfected in the instruction *as I go*!

What this means is, the more I am transformed into the image of Christ through obedience and patience, the more anointed I become for effectively performing my divine assignment.

Now, all of my "sufferings" make sense! My life's experiences have taught me a lot about people, certainly; but, more importantly, a great deal about myself!

Most of my life, I blamed others for my bad attitude, disgruntled disposition, and even for not having true friends! This truly limited my possibilities.

Now, I've learned that, although I did suffer some mistreatment, I was responsible for how I responded to

I have learned that, when an event or controversy occurs in my life, I have a split second to make the right decision: I can either be angry and go in a shell, or I can refuse to take it personal and approach the situation in a mature manner. The

people. For instance, not being allowed to go over my friend's house did not mean I had to be snappy and give everyone the silent treatment.

Not getting my way at home did not constitute me having sex with any guy who spoke what I thought I needed to hear.

I have learned that, when an event or controversy occurs in my life, I have a *split second* to make the right decision: I can either be angry and go in a shell, or I can refuse to take it personal and approach the situation in a mature manner. The choice is *always* clear, and it's always *mine*!

Opting to be angry and go in a shell is not only immature, but it also stunts your progress in life; thus hindering you from fulfilling your divine purpose for living!

The Bible declares in Matthew 6, verse 24 that *"No man can serve to masters: for either he will hate the one, and love the other; or else he will hold to the one, and despise the other. Ye cannot serve God and mammon."*

What this scripture tells us is, either you will listen to the voice of reason (the divine decision), or you will obey the voice of delusion (the pleasure of flesh); but, you most certainly can't do both.

The pleasure you feel when you retaliate, tell people off, or intentionally cause harm to others only lasts for a moment. What's worse is, the more you choose the wrong response, the more dull your sensitivity to guilt and shame becomes.

You cannot say you love the Lord and belong to Him while you make yourself feel good in the times of adversity.

The Bible in Proverbs 24 verse 10 also declares that *"If thou faint in the day of adversity, thy strength is small."* So, choosing to respond negatively indicates you have little or no faith in God, which is the source of the joy of the Lord within!

I have learned that I must be brutally honest with and about myself in order to be in right standing with and grow in the Lord.

A mature follower of righteousness does not justify their actions. You hate what the Lord hates, which includes my own displeasing ways!

I discovered that I tend to magnify others' faults to get the light off of my own. More often than not, I would rant about someone else's error as if they were satan himself for long periods of time, but expect and plead for mercy when my error(s) are revealed.

To magnify my point, I tell the following example often as it perfectly depicts our aptness to consider our own ways as right over the ways of others.

I was talking to this woman who is a Christian. When I looked down at her feet, I noticed she had on peep-toe shoes. Since she was an older woman, I thought to myself, *"Now, she knows better than to have her toe out like that. She shouldn't try to be young so she can teach the young people something."*

Immediately after talking to her, I went in the restroom. As I was coming out of the bathroom, I looked in the mirror to check my clothes. When I looked at my feet, I had on some black, dress sandals and *all* my toes were out.

I stopped in my tracks and said, "Oh Lord! Forgive me Jesus!"

This taught me that, often we are really unfair and unjust towards each other as saints! We'll take away the liberty that the Lord has freely given to all, while giving ourselves merciful leniency.

So, sometimes now when I think of that example, I wonder what was in my subconscious. In the back of my mind, did I think I was okay to have my toes (my entire feet actually) out because I was young, but when older people have their toes out they're wrong?

Perhaps I thought I was more saved than she was, so she needed to be taught a more holy way? Whatever the case may have been, (because I really don't know), my demeanor was not pleasing to the Lord in that it was like that of the *religious* Pharisees and Sadducees!

Now, I make it a point to pound it into myself to always consider myself when dealing with and relating to others.

> *I strive daily to get an understanding about me – a self awareness! That helps me to know that, if I have trouble understanding me, I most certainly need more help understanding others!*

There's no worse judgment than that which comes back to you as a result of how you have judged others.

The Bible in Proverbs 4:7 further declares that *"Wisdom is the principle thing; therefore get wisdom: and with all thy getting get an understanding."*

I strive daily to get an understanding about me – a *self* awareness! That helps me to know that, if I have trouble understanding me, I most certainly need more help understanding others!

This has helped me to possess the trust of my husband, the unfailing love of my children, and the positive, ever-building relationships of those around me.

I am more stable in character now than I've ever been in my life! I know who I am, what I'm doing and where I'm going now, for the most part. And, what I don't know doesn't crush me; rather, my lack makes me seek the Lord for the substance.

My mistakes don't control or overwhelm me. When something doesn't go as planned or expected, I often say, "*Sorry! It was a good idea!"* (It was a good idea means it seemed good when it came to my mind to do it.)

And, as the song says, *"I'm stronger! Wiser! Better! So much better!"*

Now, I have the wisdom to know that Jesus is the perfect, flawless man, not me. This awareness keeps me in a steady strive and mindset so that my flaws don't flood me.

I receive help without feeling vulnerable. I am able to look past others' countenance and allow the Lord to use me to meet their need. All that I do is no longer all about me and how I may benefit from the outcome…it's all about others *for real*!

Now, I strive to be as Paul commanded us through the Spirit of God: *"Be ye therefore followers of God as dear children."* Ephesians 5:1

In this, the sky is no longer my Limit; but, now I am L*imitless*!

*To be a
better you is to
see others better!*
What changes will
you make to
become a better
you?

NOTES

CONCLUSION

A nd finally, Sydney Smith tells us that men seldom eulogize the wisdom and virtues of their fathers, but to excuse some folly or wickedness of their own.

The Bible speaks of this idea of generational effect in Jeremiah 31:29 on this wise: *"In those days they shall say no more, The fathers have eaten a sour grape, and the children's teeth are set on edge."*

In other words, I'm unable to blame my wrong actions in life on anyone other than myself. Therefore, I live in a daily consciousness that I must exemplify a life that is worth mimicking.

Since I've become more aware of myself, I've also gained the understanding of just how frail I am in the hands of the Lord. I realize that, if it *wasn't* for the Lord, my *misery* story would have been a lot worse!

I can either have a very lonely pity party, or a lifelong, crowded celebration! I **choose** the latter!!!

Well, that's the short version of *my* story!

What about you? I was inspired to write this to encourage others to be proud of and make their boast in the Lord about their story!

What is your take away from this book? I know that *you* have a victorious story too! Please share your thoughts about this book and/or *your* story summary with me on Facebook, Twitter, Instagram, Flickr, Google+, Vimeo, or email your story summary to whocanhtbh@yahoo.com! I would love to hear from you!

Elect Lady Deirdre Cunningham serves along beside her husband, Apostle Kevin Cunningham, as the Co-Pastor at:

Vision Of Victory Evangelistic Ministries

7414 South Cottage Grove

Chicago, Illinois 60619

(773)783-8681

Contact the ministry to request
Elect Lady Deirdre Cunningham
for ministry events.

Feel free to visit and experience her ministry and the love of God within her at any time!

You may also find them on the web at:

www.visionofvictory.us

www.facebook.com/visionofvictoryevangelis

ticministries

From Limited To Limitless is the true, brief synopsis of the life of Deirdre Cunningham. Deirdre reveals how her life started out as the perfect but not so perfect childhood, but took a turn once she became of age where she thought she knew all the answers.

Just when it seemed all hope may have been lost, Deirdre discovers her life after mistakes and pitfalls.

Deirdre encourages her audience to read this book and be prompted to share this book, as well as their motivating life story to others in order to spread the epidemic of *choosing to be happy*.

Or give this book to a teenager who is struggling with issues, but wants to release themselves from the trap!

About The Author

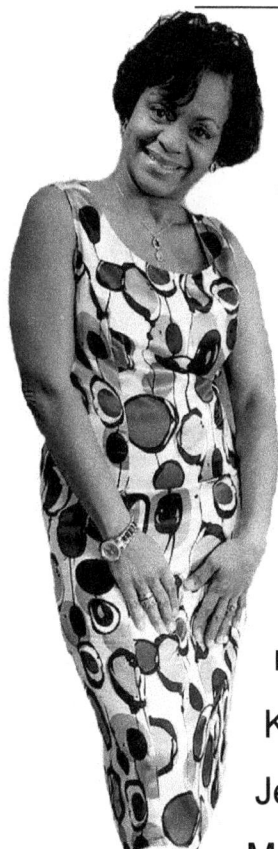

Elect Lady Deirdre Cunningham is the wife of Apostle Kevin Cunningham, Founder and Senior Pastor at Vision Of Victory Evangelistic Ministries in Chicago, IL. She is the mother of 5 children – Keith, Kara, Keaera, Kiya and Jeremiah. She is also the Mother, confidante, counselor and friend to many. She understands struggle, and with that understanding is able to pour in strength to any one ready to receive! Lady Deirdre's prayer is that the perfect love of God destroys all gloom enough to overwhelm you for the rest of your life!